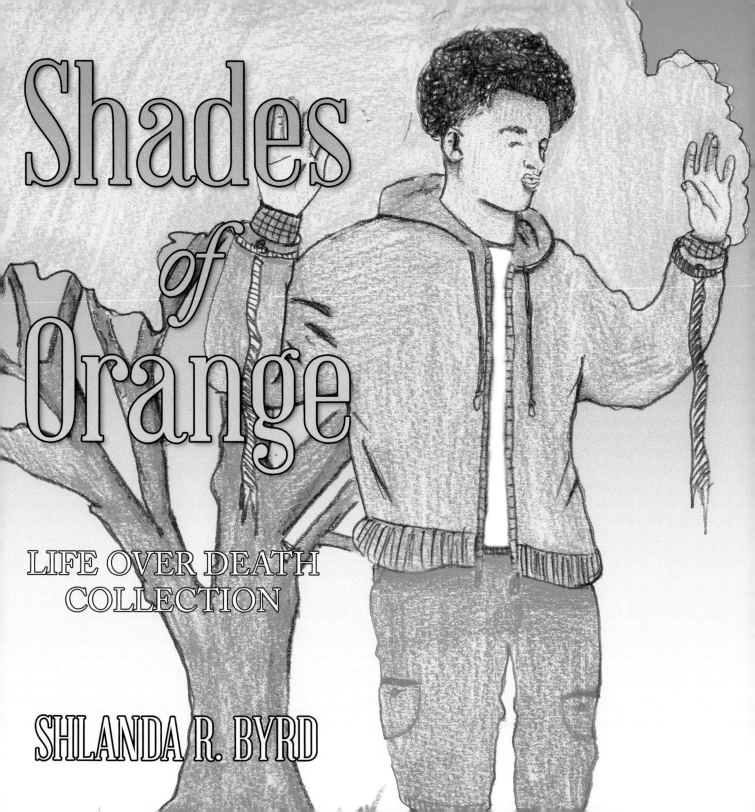

Shades
of
Orange

LIFE OVER DEATH
COLLECTION

SHLANDA R. BYRD

Scripture quotations are from the Good News
Bible © 1994 published by the Bible Societies/
HarperCollins Publishers Ltd UK, Good News Bible
© American Bible Society 1966, 1971, 1976, 1992.
Used with permission.

To order additional copies of this book, contact:
Xlibris
844-714-8691
www.Xlibris.com
Orders@Xlibris.com

ISBN: 978-1-6698-2800-6 (sc)
ISBN: 978-1-6698-2799-3 (e)

Print information available on the last page

Rev. date: 06/08/2022

Shades of Orange
Life over Death Collection
Written for the Male Child

by

Shlanda R. Byrd

My Letter to the Young Black Man

I See Your Future Secured

I know what you're thinking: "Life just ain't fair." I see you. You're just standing there on the corner, and pull your pants up. Why do you look so lost, awaiting, and in despair? I know life ain't funny for a young black man, trying to make money and questioned by authorities on every hand. Are you thirteen, fifteen, or seventeen? You appear older than your age. Is there no one to guide you? You just wander, waiting to be caught in a cage, like a slave. A cage created by human hands, guided through Satan's commands, to lock you up and throw away the key. A mature mind is what you need. Come now!

Why wander through life, when wisdom calls? Without your recollection, the wandering of an idle mind causes you to stumble and fall. You're set as a young gazelle stripped from its flock. With no one to warn you, they'll hunt you for props, gain that is. Come on, young black man. You don't need to carry a gun. If you don't awaken, and quick, prey is what you will become. Listen to wisdom, listen carefully. Follow me now; do it prayerfully. No looking backward, no time to waste. Hurry, young black man, let's escape, this way!

Separated from your purpose, your future begins to storm, thundering and lightning raining down from an unjust society. Systems are in play. You ignorantly stay in a position that causes you more harm and brings even much more pain. Hasn't anyone ever told you that Jesus is the way? I see you snatch away from the police. Son, it's a setup. Please hold your peace. Mind your manners! Where is your temperance, your respect for authorities? I know you've been taught better. "Has it all been swallowed up, given to a world's system dedicated for its tomorrow?" I ask myself.

He stumbles through life, not knowing what choices to make, or even who he looks like, abandoned. The fathers of this generation have gone astray, leaving prison systems in play. A system leaving his child to waste away, the young black man. What's in your backpack you carry so concealed, and with mischief? Are drugs and violence the only things that gratify your being? How long will you fall for paths that damage your soul? The most precious thing in life anyone can hold, far more costly than diamonds or rubies, drugs, money, designer jeans, Versace, or Gucci.

He's in darkness. Light, appear! They profit from your death, young black man, the wicked! God, is there no guidance for him from someplace? Where are the Sons of God torched with the fire and the Word to set him ablaze? I watch your life be set up, slaughtered, and untold. Your body lies slain, your blood engraved in the streets, as protesters march, shouting, "no justice, no peace." No voice to speak for you beyond the grave. I watch your generation become impoverished and enslaved, from inequality. Bondmen desiring to be free. I no longer watch but pray earnestly. Lord, turn this situation around, cause iniquity set from the enemy to cease! I speak life into your internal being, young black man. Empty of yourself! Don't drown in misery, tortured by defeat. You can allow Jesus to lead you, while you take the backseat. Do it quickly—wisdom waits!

Will he make it to his future or finish to see the bride he has chosen, and his offspring to be? From the looks, he yet wanders, displaced, ignorantly. Unaware of what to do next, he just exists, waiting to see what his life will seemingly turn out to be. No, not on my watch! This is where I draw the line. I take the lead. No more seeing and on-looking for me. I repent for watching with looks of dismay, and only praying when something happens today, tomorrow, yesterday. How sad!

Grief set upon me! I became its victim as it paralyzed, leaving me stunned. I could not speak, no sudden movements. I'm just as guilty, young black man. Guilty as I can be! I should have taken spiritual authority, commanding death to get up and flee. I allowed you to become lost, searching, and drifting in defeat. With nowhere to run, you and a baby momma carried a gun. No, my son, that ain't the one! Come now, young black man, come taste and see, while wisdom yet calls. I forbid you not from this gift of life, no, not at all. You see, life was made available for both you and me.

I can't deny you of your right to be, partaker with Christ. Jesus has much work in the kingdom of heaven. Let us both take a seat. I promise, life will get much better, just you wait and see.

I prophesy to your future, young black man. A mother for you, I will be. I take of mine own, to make you free. Here, I give you my hand, and wisdom from my mouth, a shoulder to cry on, and even my couch. I recover all! "You will not be greedy for gain. You shall not die but live. You shall prosper still, even in the midst of your mistakes. You shall not give up! Your future is secured through Jesus Christ. There shall be no violence in your stand, nor drugs in your hand, but God's plan, young black man. It will carry you over into your future. You are purposed for destiny, and God's glory shall be revealed. You shall accomplish all; death and the grave must be still." Jesus silenced that for you. You have the victory!

I decree today that graves are closing, and death has declined. No more obituaries and T-shirts designed. You are first and foremost planted singly within the family, intentionally. Now break that curse existing. Rid it from our family tree. Permanently break it and do it consistently, down through the generations of time. Young black man, pass the test and do it every time. A curse breaker is what you will be. I speak! No more readings from the earth's family, interpreting RIP to the lost young G.

No longer will you be captives, slaves to violence or fear. Neither will you be given over into the hands of plagues, curses, and disasters as time draws near. I strip you from every gutless society. You will not be detained, neither given to wicked devices, gunned down to be named. Your purpose shall remain! I watch over you, but not consumed in grief, not this time. I won't hold my peace, camouflaged with fear. In my obedience to God, I stand beside you. I give you my prayers to lead and guide you. This will cause you to be. Life over death is what I speak, as I watch God change your life forever, purposely guiding your feet. Your future, O generations, is secured through Jesus Christ and the obedience of me! *I love you!*

A Generation Refusing to Let Die

Never Give Up!

Dedicated in Memory of Keira Cortez Byrd

Psalms Chapter 14

The Good News Translation

Fools say to themselves, "There is no God!" They are all corrupt, and they have done terrible things; there is no one who does what is right. The Lord looks down from heaven to see if there are any who are wise, any who worship him. But they are all gone wrong; they are all equally bad. Not one of them does what is right, not a single one. "Don't they know?" asks the Lord. "Are all these evildoers ignorant? They live by robbing my people, and they never pray to me." But then they will be terrified, for God is with those who obey him. Evildoers frustrate the plans of the humble, but the Lord is their protection. How I pray that victory will come to Israel from Zion. How happy the people of Israel will be when the Lord makes them prosperous again!

A LIFE OVER DEATH
COLLECTION

Shades of Orange

Written for the Male Child

Hannah, a wife filled with grief, was barren, unable to give her husband a child. I can imagine how Hannah must have felt when her husband bore children to another women. He had a second wife. Her name was Peninnah. The disgrace, embarrassment, and shame Hannah must have felt as Peninnah and her children made fun of her barrenness (1 Sam. 1:7). Desperate and in need of relief, Hannah prayed, "God, if you give me a man child, I will give him back unto you all the days of his life" (1 Sam. 1:11). It was often stated that a male child took away reproach. God honored Hannah by remembering her womb. He took away her reproach of shame, in giving her a son to name Samuel.

Amale child is a greater gift to his parents. It is through him that their name and legacy lives on to be fulfilled. Abraham begat Isaac, Isaac begat Jacob, Jacob begat Joseph, and the legacy goes on and on. What a gift of double honor, God's gift of a son! What joy it brings in seeing your future generations spring forth, right before your very eyes. You train, you shape, you reprove, you correct, knowing someday, this will be the one who succeeds you after death. They hold your position in life, even after your departure: "This is my beloved son, in whom I am well pleased" (Matt. 3:17). Carry on, my son, carry on!

A son, I must prepare. It is without question, the things he must face. I must get him ready! Born in the shades of sin and shaped in iniquity, he bears the darker skin as his mother and I do. We hope earnestly, looking toward the sky, praying, "God, will you lead him that he will not die! Prepare my son, for the world ahead awaits, shaded with its colors of orange. Hurry, in this, you cannot be late!"

Shade is identified as comparative darkness and coolness caused by shelter from direct sunlight. It equates with the mind of a man tainted by the devil's hand, shaded, and threatened with fear. They even marched to Golgotha, Jesus, the Christ. The son of the Most High God was given up to die. Free Barabbas, they said as they rested Him on Calvary's hill; between two thieves is where he gave up the ghost, to lie still. He wasn't even exempt! How wicked, evil, and filled with fear, those enemies of our Lord! They feared the next man's progression in succession, succeeding them in time, as it drew near.

The mind of a man is the driving force behind the wheel of a car. I guess that's why it's always up for grabs, the devil's targeting arena for play. Joyce Myers identified it as the Battlefield of the Mind. This explains David crying out to God from the darkness of his heart through prayer: "Lord, create in me a clean heart, and renew a right spirit within me!" (Ps. 51:10). Darkness is cast out as God's light appears. The treachery and false images, the demise the devil paints on the minds of individuals through fear—it's in his thinking.

Undermining mischief, madness, and strife is a part of a plan to control. This is what Satan wants, the right to govern your life through his strongholds. Right there is the spirit that gives birth to illusions, driving every behavior that brings forth desired outcomes. Spellbound, if I must say! A mind under the devil's influence is what's happening today. Isolating me to keep me bound, telling me lies that I will forsake to swim and drown. Many don't even put up a fight. Given to evil, they fulfill every plight.

The shades of orange, so delicately painted by trickery. Uproars are created: bitterness, hatred, jealousy, and envy. Now there it goes, death over life. The kingdom of darkness is exposed. "Kill a man! It will make us rich, pure witchery!" Evil men, this is what they represent, in hunt after life, leaving only death to benefit. Hell enlarges itself daily. Violence, police brutality, politics, lies, the schemes, plots, murders, and injustice all set in disguise. Works planted to keep a shaded generation from their attempts, pursuing life, expanding, and being promoted with more benefits.

"Crucify him!" An early departure is what some say. "Death, take his life, it must be done today!" They hold a man bound to strip him of his crown, his glory. What a pity, Satan causing strife, raised in his attempt to form death over life. Wake up, somebody! Come out of a cycle repeating; you still sleeping? Not so Satan, Jesus handled that, His blood reveals it is finished, and that's a matter of fact! Come closer, my son, let me show you what to do. Time is drawing near! Take, eat this Word, the bread of life that has been broken for you. Let prayer be your cup, drink from it, it will sustain you. Just know Satan lingers near; whatever you do, *have no fear!*

An article reading characterized the color of orange as provoking immediate reactions (Stewart, Jessica 2019). "He's destroying us, what must we do? Bound a man, refrain him, keep him from his pursuits!" Fear caused them to rid him of his strength. Samson was bound by his enemies and stripped of his sight. They did everything they could in keeping him from his might. They bribed Delilah. She shaved his hair; with a razor in her hand, she left him bare. No more violent, what else could he do?

Samson was called for sport in colors of amusement, orange. Not God's weapon sent to strip those of you, enemies of our Lord! Little did they know, in the midst of their show, that God would give Samson His strength even once more. Purpose driven beyond his mistakes, Samson's hair began to grow. His purpose did not die, but he did with his final blow. Oh, how he slaughtered, ordained in strength. The enemies of the Lord were stilled; they lost all their benefits, including their lives.

Behold, the Son of Righteousness shall return in the midst of wicked men, clothed in a generation of deception, greed, and tales within. On the wings of the clouds the Son will ride, but know Satan has fallen, tempting and in disguise. Be not deceived, my son, for his motives are not pure. Even though it sounds tempting, don't forget what I have taught you! Be wise, my son, attend to my instructions. You never know where Satan's lurking in wait, or who he will use yet. Always remember, he is a snake. Remain focused that you may surpass the deceptions. Fly with the eagles, strive for excellence. God will strengthen you, above and beyond measure. Fulfill, my son, our legacy free from sin, which our God has secured for us. Stay faithful until the end!

Why are my son's hands tied, held bound by the wrists? Is he your human sacrifice? Why, Jesus paid for this! He wears the shaded colors of orange. A threat to you, being held back, he cannot resist. "My jacket, my pants, my shirt?" He asks the question. "I'm only thirteen, held down. What does this mean? Oh, how it hurts!" He takes notice of his wrists bound, the shaded colors of orange clothing surrounding him. It's OK, my son. Suffer only for a short time with me. After a while, you will be free, you'll see.

They nailed Jesus to a cross, bound by the wrists, just as you, my son, but he did not resist. Their goal was to keep him from fulfilling what he was sent to do; instead, they fulfilled, in giving life back to you. You were sent here with a purpose, greater than you and I. Jesus secured it—that's why he was sent to die. You see, my son, Christ knew you would be born into a world filled with adversity. He reassured your success with his death. He made living worth it! Born with a purpose to fulfill, he was ready to die. His death freed your wrists from being bound by the color of your skin, the orange clothing you were suited in, the yoke tied around your neck, the guilt, shame, and neglect. The idleness of your hands, your inability to take a stand, the fear of living in defeat, the regret of watching others take the seat. Jesus has released you without limits. Nothing they do can keep you bound. Go ahead, son, finish, wear your crown.

Be who you were born to be. Accomplish what you are sent to accomplish. Go ahead. It's OK. You don't have to be afraid. It's your time to shine now! The Holy Spirit will comfort and guide you, every step of the way. You are released to flourish. Though you have been held back, that you don't have to worry about. Live your purpose! Stop pondering in yesterdays. Remember, the just shall live by faith. Get ready to receive double, now escalate!

Wear your mantle, my son, and wear it well. It's your anointing! A garment chosen for you, and it's not for sale. It's no time for competing, no time to be conceited. Purge yourself of evil thoughts that can block you in advancing, from achieving. Let these words renew your mind. Fight the good fight of faith, pass the test every time. Whatever your hands find to do, do it with all your might. The angels and I are watching, cheering you through every plight, your light.

Carry on, my son, accomplish, serve God well. You press for our future! The Lord has appointed you, and he will not leave my soul in hell; neither will he suffer his holy one to see corruption! Take away my reproach, my male child. With you I shall accomplish, though I must rest a while. Through you, my legacy lives on infinitely, without the numbering of days. I have been given a chance to live on, life beyond the grave. A life without ending is what Jesus has finished for you and me. In generations fulfilling, we arise to fruition, completing our mission, and ain't no time for quitting. We are purposed to fulfill, so *live and not die!*

"My Letter to You, My Male Child"

The End

Who Are You?

_____

_____

_____

_____

_____

_____

_____

_____

Know Who You Are

So God created man in his own image, in the image of God created he him; male and female created He them. And God blessed them, and God said unto them, "Be fruitful, and multiply, and replenish the earth, and subdue it: and have dominion over the fish of the sea, and over the fowl of the air, and over every living thing that moveth upon the earth." (Gen. 1:27)

Then the word of the Lord came unto me, saying, "Before I formed thee in the belly I knew thee; and before thou camest forth out of the womb I sanctified thee, and I ordained thee a prophet unto the nations." (Jer. 1:5)

You Were Born to Accomplish

O Lord, our Lord, how excellent is thy name in all the earth! Who hast set the glory above the heavens? Out of the mouth of babes and sucklings hast thou ordained strength because of thine enemies, that thou mightest still the enemy and the avenger. When I consider thy heavens, the work of thy fingers, the moon and the stars, which thou hast ordained; What is man, that thou art mindful of him? And the son of man, that thou visitest him? For thou hast made him a little lower than the angels and has crowned him with glory and honor. Thou madest him to have dominion over the works of thy hands; thou hast put all things under his feet: sheep and oxen, Yea, and the beasts of the field, the fowl of the air, and the fish of the sea, and whatsoever passeth through the paths of the seas. O Lord, our Lord, how excellent is thy name in all the earth! (Ps. 8)

What Is Your Purpose?

_____

_____

_____

_____

_____

_____

_____

You Are Anointed to Prosper

"The Spirit of the Lord God is upon me, because the Lord hath anointed me to preach good tidings unto the meek; he hath sent me to bind up the brokenhearted, to proclaim liberty to the captives, and the opening of the prison to them that are bound; to proclaim the acceptable year of the Lord, and the day of vengeance of our God; to comfort all that mourn; to appoint unto them that mourn in Zion, to give unto them beauty for ashes, the oil of joy for mourning, the garment of praise for the spirit of heaviness; that they might be called trees of righteousness, the planting of the Lord, that he might be glorified. And they shall build the old wastes, they shall rise up the former desolations, and they shall repair the waste cities, the desolations of many generations. And strangers shall stand and feed your flocks, and the sons of the alien shall be your plowmen and your vinedressers. But ye shall be named Priests of the Lord: men shall call you the Ministers of our God: ye shall eat the riches of the Gentiles, and in their glory shall ye boast yourselves. For your shame ye shall have double; and for confusion they shall rejoice in their portion: therefore in their land they shall possess the double: everlasting joy shall be unto them. For I the Lord love judgment, I hate robbery for burnt offerings; and I will direct their work in truth, and I will make an everlasting covenant with them. And their seed shall be known among the Gentiles, and their offspring among the people; all that see them shall acknowledge them, and they are the seed which the Lord hath blessed. I will greatly rejoice in the Lord, my soul shall be joyful in my God; for he hath clothed me with the garments of salvation, he hath covered me with the robe of righteousness, as a bridegroom decketh himself with ornaments, and as a bride adorneth herself with her jewels. For as the earth bringeth forth her bud, and as the garden causeth the things that are sown in it to spring forth; so the Lord God will cause righteousness and praise to spring forth before all the nations." (Isa. 61)

Are You Positioned to Fulfill Purpose?

_____

_____

_____

_____

_____

How Can You Get There?

_____

_____

_____

_____

_____

Now the Lord said to Abraham, "Get thee out of thy country, and from thy kindred, and from thy father's house, unto a land that I will shew thee: and I will make thee a great nation and I will bless thee, and make thy name great; and thou shalt be a blessing: and I will bless them that bless thee, and curse them that curse thee: and in thee shall all the families of the earth be blessed." So Abraham departed, as the Lord had spoken unto him. (Gen. 12:1–4)

Guided to Reign in Dominion and Power

Now after the death of Moses the servant of the Lord, it came to pass that the Lord spoke unto Joshua the son of Nun, Moses' minister, saying, "Moses my servant is dead; now therefore arise, go over the Jordan, thou, and all this people, unto the land which I do give them, even to the children of Israel. Every place that the sole of your foot shall tread upon, that have I given unto you, as I said to Moses. From the wilderness and this Lebanon even unto the great river Euphrates, all the land of the Hittites, and unto the great sea toward the going down of the sun shall be your coast. There shall not any man be able to stand before thee all the days of thy life: as I was with Moses, so will I be with thee. I will not fail thee, nor forsake thee. Be strong and of good courage: for unto this people shalt thou divide for an inheritance the land, which I sware unto their fathers to give them. Only be thou strong and very courageous, that thou mayest observe to do according to all the law, which Moses my servant commanded thee: turn not from it to the right hand or to the left, that thou mayest prosper whithersoever thou goest. Have not I commanded thee? Be strong and of a good courage; be not afraid, neither be thou dismayed; for the Lord thy God is with thee whithersoever thou goest." (Josh. 1:1–9)

Blessed or Cursed

A family tree wears either a curse or a blessing

Jesus took off His garment of righteousness and traded with us, becoming "the curse of a tree."

INCERTATION
The Significance of the Cross and the Bound Male Child

Breaking Family Curses

In the beginning, God gave a command. "Obey me" were His words securing the life in which we stand, all in his plan to prosper us. Before God could turn his head in just a few, Satan was showing up, telling us what to do, reversing God's order, confusing us in every way. We sat and listened to what Satan had to say. His wickedness, the temptations in our weakness are what led us astray. Blind, we entered a curse. This tree you see pictured, it stripped us in wearing the blessings. Dressed in my father's name, tagged in shades of orange surrounding me, my wrists are bound. Satan has robbed us from wearing our crown, in fulfilling destiny.

P ut here on earth to prosper in every way, we died listening to what the devil had to say. Our purpose, our righteous way of life, swallowed within minutes; we begin walking in pride. The enemy planted his spirit, deceitfully winning. He filled us with strife and led away our life. Murderer, adulterer, liar, and thief, this was the blaze that filled us with grief. Bad fruit grew from our tree, Satan's characteristics. No life, you see! It separated us from God. Yes, we were banished, sent away from His presence. God having to recover us, he raised up a plan. It would cleanse our stains from deception, and it had to be done through man. A plan, in allowing us to return to him forever, again. All God asked us to do was obey!

The wooden tree in my rear view reveals the scares they did know, my ancestors. The thick bark upon its trunk was the darkness covered. Tinted was its shade of orange giving coolness to its deceit. A covering for abominable acts became quite scary to me. I carried grief concealed within, from what I discovered. My uncle was really my brother, hidden. I was betrayed by what I perceived to be true. In a false image is where hatred began to brew. The things hidden in the dark, deep roots, keep me in agony, resenting. A family grew apart. Curses from way back when reoccurred over and over again. They're hitting me, even still today! A tree trunk so great I carry its weight, and with scares, a curse.

Granddaddy struggled, daddy, uncles, now me too. Their disobedience led them in chasing desires out the blue! Overtaken in evil desires, they let fear win. All initiated at the hand of Satan, he ain't nobody's friend! Filling you with lies, he uses whoever he can. Full of fear, what else is left for a black male to do? Cry, surrender quietly, and repeat the cycle too! Those before me didn't get very far. They gave themselves to familiar spirits, all lies, of course. Robbed of the blessings our fathers had to gain. Living in strife under the hand of the enemy has driven men insane, moonstruck by night. A curse, Satan left it as he walked away with our blessings. He set the course in motion, seeking to exalt himself. He tainted us all with his evil spirit; it kept iniquity in our linage. My wrists are bound. Now, it is left up to me!

"Cursed is everyone who hangeth on a tree," is found within the scriptures of Galatians 3:13. My son, one day I'll see. A curse for him, I forbid it to be, only the blessings. I vow my life so diligently, breaking the curse from my family tree, for my son and generations to be. My life I commit in surrendering it all. I surrender it now. I take Jesus. Lord, don't let me fall! I refuse to be bound! Messiah, free my wrists! I want to live again, even after this. Christ has redeemed us from the curse of the law, being made a curse for us, that the blessings might be released. Jesus fulfilled in trading my place for His. He took away me being bound to a tree. A wooden cross he carried, they bound him to that tree. They bound him, his hands and his feet. A curse he became,

He died, for you and me. An heir, and a joint heir with Christ, I became. A curse no more a part of my family's name, but blessings.

God is in the generations of the righteous: "Praise ye the Lord. Blessed is the man that feareth the Lord, that delighteth greatly in His commandments. His seed shall be mighty upon earth: the generations of the upright shall be blessed. Wealth and riches shall be in his house: and his righteousness endureth forever" (Ps. 112:1–4). I once was bound, but Christ has made me and my family free. He did it all, on the earth's family tree. Generations are free! In him, the families of the earth are blessed. Now walk in it!

Wear the blessings through obedience—it seats you in heavenly places!

You are royal priesthoods!

Wear your crown, king!

I niquity passed down through generations produces dead branches, unproductiveness.

The curse is initiated through acts of disobedience to God, reproducing negative cycles repeating themselves. Bondage

When a father chooses to walk in obedience to God, no matter the iniquity of the fathers before, his tree begins to change for the next generations. Fruitful branches appear.

The son is positioned better than his father. His father set him up to succeed by securing his life in obedience to God. Though you do see negative patterns attempt to reoccur, this is due to iniquity in the family lineage. However, the outcome of the son is more rewarding than that of his father before. The father gets the opportunity he never had through his son living. This could not have been done without the father willingly submitting to the obedience of God for both him and his son. They become foundation layers of righteousness for future generations.

Jesus is king of kings and lord of lords!

Christal Became the Curse

Christ was wounded for our transgressions; He was bruised for our iniquities: the chastisement of our peace was upon Him, and with His stripes we are healed. (Isa. 53:5)

In Jesus Christ, the families of the earth are blessed through righteousness. No longer are they under a curse, but blessings!

The blood of Jesus has washed away our stains and iniquities carried upon our family tree.

The blessings are released!

Time to Fulfill Purpose

The shades of orange no longer have you held down, bound by the wrists.
These were Jesus's final words:
"It is finished!"
No weapon formed against you shall prosper!
You prosper, live and not die, life over death!
Fulfill the future of dreams, for generations of tomorrow.

Printed in the United States
by Baker & Taylor Publisher Services